A BUSINESS APPROACH TO AVOCADO FARMING

Complete Entrepreneurial Step By Step Guide To Avocado Garden From Scratch

I0427340

ZHURI HART

DISCLAIMER

This book is intended to provide general information and insights on adopting a business approach to farming. The content within is based on the author's knowledge and experiences up to the date of publication. It is essential to recognize that the field of agriculture is dynamic, influenced by various factors such as market conditions, climate, and regulatory changes.

Readers are advised to conduct thorough research, seek professional advice, and consider their unique circumstances before implementing any strategies or practices discussed in this book. The author and publisher disclaim any responsibility for the accuracy, completeness, or suitability of the information provided. The book is not a substitute for professional advice, and the author and publisher shall not be liable for any damages or losses arising from the use or reliance on the information presented herein.

Individual results may vary, and success in farming enterprises is contingent upon numerous variables. The author encourages readers to consult with relevant experts, agricultural extension services, and legal or financial professionals to tailor strategies to their specific needs and local conditions.

This book is not intended to be a comprehensive guide to all aspects of farming, and readers should exercise their judgment and discretion in applying the principles discussed. The author and publisher do not endorse any specific products, services, or companies mentioned in this book unless explicitly stated.

By reading this book, the reader acknowledges and accepts the inherent uncertainties in agricultural endeavors and agrees to use the information at their own risk.

TABLE OF CONTENTS

ABOUT THE BOOK

"A Business Approach to Avocado Farming," a book, provides a thorough overview for those who want to start or expand their avocado farming business. Setting the scene, the introduction explores the history of avocado farming, emphasizes its importance in the market, and outlines the goals of the book.

An overview of the avocado market's fundamentals, including market dynamics, trends, opportunities, and problems, is given. Making wise judgments and managing the difficulties of the avocado-growing industry require this expertise.

Planning and market research are essential components of any successful business, and they are covered in detail. To help readers perform market research, pinpoint potential clients, and create a solid business strategy that is specific to the peculiarities of avocado farming, the book adopts a methodical approach.

The significance of choosing the appropriate avocado types is discussed, with a focus on popular varieties, selection-influencing factors, and market demand analysis. Readers will leave this chapter with the knowledge necessary to make strategic decisions in line with consumer preferences and market trends.

The intricacies of starting and maintaining avocado orchards are explored in depth, where topics including choosing a site, designing the orchard, planting trees, pruning, irrigation, and pest control are covered. These sections offer practical insights into the daily activities that are essential to the well-being and efficiency of avocado farms.

Examines the crucial stages of harvesting, post-harvest processing, and storage. Maintaining avocado quality and making sure they are ready for the market requires understanding when is the best time to harvest, using appropriate harvesting methods, and controlling post-harvest procedures.

The book move beyond cultivation and concentrate on financial management and marketing, respectively. The information that readers learn about creating a brand, creating successful marketing campaigns, comprehending sales channels, estimating expenses, budgeting, financial planning, and evaluating return on investment is invaluable.

The book focuses on sustainability as it comes to an end. It covers the growing consumer demand for sustainable agricultural products, the advantages of sustainable and organic avocado production, and the complexities of organic certification and methods.

"A Business Approach to Avocado Farming" offers a realistic, business-oriented viewpoint that transcends the theoretical components of farming. This book is a valuable tool for anyone looking to succeed in the avocado sector because it covers all aspects of the growing process, from sustainability to marketing.

CHAPTER ONE

INTRODUCTION TO AVOCADO FARMING

HISTORY OF AVOCADO CULTIVATION

Throughout several historical periods and geographical locations, avocado cultivation has been a prominent agricultural practice. Avocados are indigenous to south-central Mexico and date back thousands of years to the time of the Aztec and Mayan civilizations. Avocados were once thought of as a rich delicacy and a fertility symbol. However, as time went on, their nutritional worth and wide range of culinary uses won them over as global icons.

Avocado growing has progressed from conventional farming techniques to cutting-edge, contemporary ways. In addition to improving production efficiency, the change in agricultural practices has helped avocado agriculture spread throughout the world. Beyond their home Mexico, several nations have emerged as major players in the avocado sector in recent decades, contributing to the industry's diversification and the growth of the avocado market worldwide.

AVOCADO'S SIGNIFICANCE IN THE MARKET

The market value of avocados is enormous since these nutrient-dense, creamy fruits are now a mainstay in many different cuisines across the globe. Avocados have become increasingly popular because of their distinct flavor, smooth texture, and several health advantages.

Avocados are known to support heart health because of their high nutrient content, which includes vital vitamins, minerals, and antioxidants, as well as their rich source of monounsaturated fats. Because of their advantageous nutritional profile, avocados are now in high demand and are often used in diets that prioritize health.

Beyond their culinary uses, avocados are incredibly versatile. Because of their natural oils and nourishing qualities, avocados have become more and more popular in beauty and skincare products as people's attention has turned to wellness and good living. Furthermore, the avocado business is vital to worldwide trade since it is exported and imported by many nations, promoting economic expansion and international agricultural collaborations.

Avocados are frequently commended in the context of sustainable agriculture for their capacity to flourish in a variety of climates, enhancing the adaptability of agricultural methods.

But the growth of avocado farming has also sparked environmental worries, especially in areas where water scarcity is a major problem. The business constantly struggles to strike a balance between the financial advantages of avocado growing and ecologically responsible methods.

Digging deeper into the world of avocado production and its market dynamics reveals that cultural, economic, and environmental factors have played a role in this creamy green fruit's path from ancient symbolism to global commodity status. Gaining knowledge about the history of avocado cultivation and the market's significance for avocados will help one better understand the complex interplay of variables influencing this booming sector.

CHAPTER TWO

COMPREHENDING THE AVOCADO SECTOR

AN OVERVIEW OF THE MARKET FOR AVOCADOS

In recent years, the avocado sector has grown and changed dramatically, establishing itself as a major player in the global market. The avocado, sometimes known as "green gold," is so versatile and full of nutrients that it has become a mainstay in diets all around the world. Because of rising consumer knowledge of the health advantages of avocados, the market for avocados has grown outside of typical avocado-producing countries.

OPPORTUNITIES AND TRENDS IN AVOCADO FARMING

The rise in demand for avocados that are cultivated organically and responsibly is one noteworthy trend in the avocado market. Growing consumer demand for products that reflect their beliefs is causing a shift in farming practices toward those that are more socially and environmentally conscious.

Because of this, there are plenty of chances for avocado farmers that use sustainable farming practices to meet customer demand and maintain the industry's long-term viability.

Furthermore, avocado farming has benefited greatly from technological improvements. Productivity and efficiency have increased thanks to advances in precision agriculture, data analytics, and creative cultivation methods.

For example, growers may monitor their avocado groves, evaluate crop health, and improve irrigation techniques by using drones and satellite photos. Adopting such technologies opens doors for more productive and economical farming, enhancing the industry's overall sustainability in the avocado sector.

OBSTACLES IN THE AVOCADO FARMING INDUSTRY

Although the avocado sector has a lot of potential, several obstacles could affect the long-term viability and profitability of avocado farms. Climate change is a serious obstacle since it might result in erratic weather patterns that have an impact on avocado production. Droughts, severe rain, or extreme temperatures can all interfere with fruit development and flowering, which could affect supply and price.

Avocado trees also face the threat of pests like the avocado lace insect and diseases like laurel wilt and root rot due to their high disease sensitivity. Avocado trees are especially susceptible, therefore finding disease-resistant types and employing efficient pest control techniques will need ongoing research and funding.

Avocado growers are likewise concerned about market volatility. Demand and supply changes in the worldwide avocado market are caused by a variety of factors, including trade regulations, exchange rates, and geopolitical developments. The income of avocado growers can be impacted by changes in market dynamics, which emphasizes the necessity for risk management techniques in the sector. Prices might also change.

Rising customer demand and technology developments are driving the avocado industry's success. Farmers do, however, confront difficulties because of diseases, unstable markets, and climate change. To maintain the long-term viability and resilience of avocado farming enterprises, navigating these obstacles demands a comprehensive strategy that incorporates cutting-edge technologies, sustainable practices, and adaptive management.

CHAPTER THREE

PLANNING AND MARKET RESEARCH

UNDERTAKING AVOCADO MARKET ANALYSIS

An in-depth look at a range of aspects is necessary to acquire a better understanding of the state of the avocado market today and what to expect in the future. This process usually entails analyzing the competitive environment, comprehending customer preferences, and assessing the dynamics of supply and demand.

It is possible to discover prospective opportunities and problems for avocado farming by analyzing market trends.

The viability and profitability of avocado farming are greatly influenced by variables like market pricing, demand in the area, and climate. A thorough market analysis also benefits from researching potential dangers and the regulatory environment.

IDENTIFYING TARGET CUSTOMERS

Determining the demographics, habits, and interests of prospective customers is a necessary step in avocado farming. Regarding avocados, consumer preferences can differ according to age, financial level, way of life, and nutritional preferences. Customer segmentation and profile creation can be aided by surveys, interviews, and data analysis. For example, because avocados are high in nutrients, those who are health-conscious might be a large target market. Furthermore, developing a diverse clientele requires an awareness of the preferences of companies like food processors, supermarkets, and restaurants. For avocado farming to be successful, marketing tactics must be specifically tailored to meet the needs and preferences of these target demographics.

MAKING A BUSINESS PLAN FOR AVOCADO FARMING

Making a business plan for avocado farming is a calculated step that entails stating the goals, strategies, and resources needed to make the endeavor successful. A thorough market study, financial forecasts, operational plans, and risk management should all be included in the strategy. A thorough business plan also covers important topics including pest management, irrigation techniques, property acquisition, and farming methods. To guarantee smooth operations, a schedule for planting, harvesting, and marketing avocados must be included. To offer a clear road map for the avocado farming endeavor, financial factors including budgeting, funding sources, and revenue estimates must also be well described. Frequent review and revision of the business plan guarantees the avocado farming business's sustained performance by enabling it to adjust to shifting market conditions.

CHAPTER FOUR

SELECTING THE BEST TYPES OF AVOCADOS

POPULAR TYPES OF AVOCADOS

It's important to take into account the variety of avocado varieties that are available on the market while selecting the best ones. Popular avocado types range in terms of flavor, texture, and climatic adaptation.

The Hass avocado is a well-known kind that is praised for its rich flavor and creamy texture. Its versatility in culinary applications—which makes it a favorite for salads and guacamole—is the reason for its popularity.

The Fuerte avocado cultivar is also worth mentioning because of its smooth, creamy texture and mildly nutty flavor. Due to their adaptability to diverse conditions, fuerte avocados are frequently preferred and may be grown in a variety of locations.

Bacon avocados stand out for their distinct flavor profile in addition to their pear-like form and buttery texture.

CONSIDERATIONS FOR VARIETY SELECTION

During the choosing process, several things need to be considered. Climate is important since different types of avocados grow best in different temperatures. Successful production requires knowledge of the local climate as well as the ideal growing conditions for the avocado kind. To guarantee ideal growth and fruit development, other environmental elements including drainage, sunlight exposure, and soil type should be taken into account.

Another thing to think about is the avocado tree's size. Certain cultivars, like Wurtz or "Little Cado," are renowned for being little and fitting for container gardening or smaller areas.

Larger cultivars, on the other hand, such as the Reed or Pinkerton, could need more room to grow to their full potential. To have a healthy avocado orchard, space availability, and planting site must be taken into account.

EVALUATING DEMAND IN THE MARKET FOR PARTICULAR VARIETIES

Furthermore, it's important to thoroughly evaluate the market demand for particular avocado kinds. Global and regional variations in consumer preferences might affect how profitable avocado farming is.

Growers can choose which types of avocados to farm by keeping up with market trends and knowing which ones are in high demand.

In addition, satisfying consumer demands and guaranteeing the financial viability of avocado farming operations depend heavily on taking into account variables like shelf life, shipping durability, and post-harvest qualities.

Choosing the best avocado cultivars requires a thorough assessment of variables such as tree size, market demand, and climate appropriateness. Growers can make well-informed decisions that support productive avocado growth and a strong market presence by being aware of the distinctive qualities of various avocado varieties and matching them with the climate and consumer preferences.

CHAPTER FIVE

HOW TO PLANT AND MAINTAIN AVOCADO ORCHARDS

CHOOSING APPROPRIATE LAND FOR GROWING AVOCADOS

Selecting the appropriate area for avocado cultivation is an essential first step toward building a productive orchard. Avocado trees grow best in well-drained soils that have a pH between 6 and 7.5. To determine the composition and nutritional content of the soil, soil tests are necessary. A prevalent problem in avocado plantations, root infections can be avoided with adequate drainage. Furthermore, choosing terrain with a small slope promotes water flow and avoids water logging, both of which can be harmful to avocado trees.

Climate is important for growing avocados; avocado trees like temperatures between 60°F and 85°F (15°C and 29°C). It's crucial to pick a spot where there is little chance of frost because avocado trees can suffer damage from it. Strong winds have the potential to hinder a tree's growth and development, thus it is important to take their direction into account as well.

DESIGN AND LAYOUT OF ORCHARDS

An avocado orchard's layout and design play a major role in maximizing output and supporting effective management techniques. The design of an orchard should include things like the distance between trees, the direction of the rows, and the accessibility of irrigation and pest management. To maximize solar exposure and promote air circulation, which helps avoid illness, trees must be spaced properly apart.

To guarantee an even distribution of sunlight, rows should be oriented to maximize their exposure to the sun. This usually means aligning rows north to south. For the sake of convenience during orchard operations and machinery transportation, rows must be spaced enough apart. Avocados are sensitive to both water excess and deficiency, thus planning for irrigation systems like drip irrigation is necessary to guarantee a steady supply of water.

GROWING AND MAINTAINING AVOCADO TREES

To guarantee good tree growth and maximum fruit output, avocado trees require meticulous attention to detail during planting and maintenance. Avocado trees are usually propagated by grafting, and the long-term health of the tree depends on the choice of high-quality rootstocks. To give the tree enough time to adjust to its new surroundings before winter, planting should ideally take place in the spring or early summer.

During the establishment phase, proper irrigation is essential, with an emphasis on continuous hydration without water logging. Mulching the area around the tree's base aids in temperature regulation, weed control, and soil moisture retention.

Frequent fertilization with a balanced mixture of nutrients, especially nitrogen, phosphorus, and potassium, is beneficial for avocado plants.

Avocado orchards require routine pest and disease monitoring. By putting integrated pest management techniques into practice, chemical pesticide usage can be reduced and the orchard's ecology can be strengthened. Another essential component of tree care is pruning, which shapes the tree to provide for maximum sunlight exposure, air circulation, and harvesting simplicity.

The construction and upkeep of avocado orchards necessitate careful consideration of several issues, including the selection of appropriate sites, the implementation of efficient orchard design and layout, and the assurance of proper planting and maintenance of avocado trees. A comprehensive strategy is necessary for long-term success and consistent fruit output in avocado cultivation.

CHAPTER SIX

MAINTENANCE OF AVOCADO TREES

AVOCADO TREE PRUNING AND TRAINING

A vital part of maintaining avocado trees is pruning, which improves the trees' health, form, and fruit yield. Pruning a tree properly promotes air circulation, increases sunshine penetration, and helps control the tree's size. Early on, avocado trees are frequently pruned to promote a robust, well-organized framework. To encourage a balanced canopy, this entails trimming away competing branches, dead wood, and undesired growth.

Guiding the growth of avocado trees to attain the optimal structure is known as training. Both central leader and open-center pruning are frequently used;

the former encourages a more spreading canopy, while the latter promotes a single, dominant trunk. Throughout the tree's life, regular trimming procedures assist preserve the shape, regulating size, and increasing fruiting efficiency. But it's important to avoid over-pruning, which can cause stress and lower fruit yield.

TECHNIQUES FOR IRRIGATING AVOCADO ORCHARDS

Due to their extreme sensitivity to water stress, avocado trees require efficient watering techniques to flourish and produce fruit at their best. Generally speaking, avocado plantations need a steady and carefully controlled water supply, particularly during important times like flowering and fruit sets. Commonly used drip irrigation systems minimize water waste by supplying water straight to the tree's root zone.

Monitoring soil moisture levels is essential for figuring out when and how much irrigation is required. Well-drained soils are ideal for avocado trees while overwatering can cause root infections. The key to effective irrigation management in avocado orchards is designing a timetable based on the water requirements of the trees, adjusting for seasonal variations, and considering weather and soil type.

CONTROLLING INSECTS AND DISEASES IN AVOCADO AGRICULTURE

Because avocado trees are vulnerable to a wide range of pests and illnesses, good management practices are essential to preserving the production and health of the orchard. The widespread application of Integrated Pest Management (IPM) techniques emphasizes the use of cultural customs, biological control, and sparing chemical application. Regular scouting for pests and pathogens aids in the early detection of problems.

Aphids, mites, and several types of beetles are common pests that harm avocado trees. Pest populations can be managed using biological management techniques including introducing natural predators like parasitic wasps or ladybugs. Disease control techniques include things like keeping ideal soil conditions, trimming properly to allow for air circulation, and, when feasible, choosing avocado kinds resistant to disease.

Fungicides can be used to prevent disease, along with treatments that target particular infections. Disease control measures also include regular orchard sanitation, eliminating diseased plant waste, and disposing of it properly. To maintain the long-term health and productivity of their orchards, avocado producers must remain updated about newly developing pests and illnesses and adjust their management tactics accordingly.

CHAPTER SEVEN

HARVESTING AND HANDLING AFTER HARVEST

CHOOSING THE APPROPRIATE TIME TO HARVEST

A crucial component of effective agricultural practices—and one that applies to avocado growing as well—is figuring out when to harvest. The fruit's nutritional value, flavor, and quality are all strongly influenced by when it is harvested. Asynchronous fruit maturity, in which different stages of fruit development coexist on the same tree, is a characteristic of avocado plants. It becomes crucial to keep an eye on the fruit's physiological characteristics, such as its skin tone, texture, and oil level, to determine when it is best to harvest it.

The choice of cultivar, the local climate, and the target market all play a part in the decision-making process. A common visual indication used by cultivators to determine when a fruit is mature is when its skin turns from green to a darker shade. Furthermore, evaluating the fruit's firmness and oil content gives important details about when it's ready to be harvested. Striking a balance between leaving the fruit on the tree to develop its full flavor and removing it early to avoid over ripening presents a problem.

METHODS FOR HARVESTING AVOCADO

Care must be used when picking avocados to prevent injury and maintain fruit quality. Because of the fruit's delicate nature, handling it gently is necessary to prevent bruising and other mechanical injuries. The best way to harvest avocados is by hand, as this enables you to pick the mature fruit only and leave the immature ones on the tree to ripen further. Depending on the size and accessibility of the tree, picking is usually done by hand climbing or using poles equipped with picking bags.

Because mechanical harvesting has the potential to harm the delicate fruit, it is not a popular practice. Avocados should be handled carefully after harvesting to avoid surface flaws and guarantee that they arrive at the market in the best possible shape. To separate fruit according to size, maturity, and quality to fulfill market standards, sorting and grading are essential procedures in the post-harvest process.

AFTER-HARVEST MANAGEMENT AND PRESERVATION

The care given to avocados after harvest is essential to preserving their quality and shelf life. To prolong the fruit's marketability and slow down the ripening process, immediate refrigeration is necessary. Because avocados are susceptible to temperature changes, controlled environment storage facilities are frequently used to control the humidity, temperature, and gas composition to extend the shelf life of avocados.

Another crucial component of post-harvest treatment is packaging, which shields the fruit from physical harm while it is being transported and stored. Fruit bruising can be avoided and overall quality preserved with the use of packing materials that support and cushion the fruit, as well as properly ventilated containers. To guarantee that avocados retain their flavor and texture until they are consumed, cold storage and transportation networks are essential. This will increase consumer satisfaction and minimize post-harvest losses.

CHAPTER EIGHT

STRATEGIES FOR MARKETING AND SALES

DEVELOPING YOUR AVOCADO BUSINESS'S BRAND

Any company that wants to succeed must have a strong, recognizable brand, and the avocado sector is no exception. Developing a distinctive value proposition, a recognizable visual identity, and consistent messaging are all essential components of brand building for avocado businesses.

Determine what makes your avocados unique from others on the market before anything else. This could have to do with your avocados' sustainability, freshness, or quality.

Create a captivating brand narrative that explains your avocados' journey from farm to table. Talk about the love and care you put into growing avocados, and highlight any eco-friendly techniques you use. A compelling brand narrative builds an emotional bond with customers that promote trust and loyalty.

Make a bold visual identity investment, incorporating a recognizable logo, color palette, and packaging. A unified and identifiable brand for your avocado business may be achieved by maintaining consistency in branding across all touch points, including product labels and your web presence. Utilize social media to interact with your audience and promote your brand's beliefs and lifestyle in addition to its products.

CREATING MARKETING CAMPAIGNS THAT WORK

Developing successful marketing strategies for your avocado business necessitates a thorough comprehension of market trends and your target demographic. To find out about customer trends, attitudes, and preferences regarding avocados, conduct market research. Make use of this data to customize your marketing tactics and messaging so that they appeal to your target market.

To reach a larger audience, think about utilizing both traditional and digital marketing platforms. Make use of social media channels to promote avocado recipes, health advantages, and interesting content. To increase your reach and reputation, work with nutrition experts and influencers.

Personalization campaigns can also be very successful. To customize your messaging, take into account segmentation based on purchasing patterns, preferences, or demographics. To assess the effectiveness of your campaigns and create data-driven improvements for ongoing progress, use data analytics.

NETWORKS OF DISTRIBUTION AND SALES CHANNELS

To guarantee that your avocados are efficiently delivered to customers, you must select appropriate sales channels and distribution networks. Examine a range of choices, such as direct-to-consumer sales, internet platforms, local marketplaces, and supermarkets. Because every channel has benefits and drawbacks, the best course of action might be to combine them strategically.

An effective distribution network requires solid partnerships with distributors and retailers. To help them sell more avocados, give them marketing materials, product details, and encouragement. To develop distinctive selling propositions in particular channels, take into account exclusive partnerships or collaborations.

A large part of your distribution plan may consist of online sales. Create an intuitive e-commerce platform and look into joint ventures with reputable online retailers. For on-time and fresh delivery, implement strong supply chain management and logistics.

Creating a strong brand, creating efficient marketing methods, and choosing the best possible sales and distribution channels are all interconnected tactics that will help your avocado business succeed.

CHAPTER NINE

MANAGING MONEY IN AVOCADO FARMING

ESTIMATING AND PLANNING COSTS

Budgeting and cost estimation are essential components of financial management in avocado cultivation. A farmer's cost of inputs, including labor, planting supplies, fertilizers, irrigation, pest control, and soil preparation, must be precisely estimated.

To ascertain the entire costs incurred during the various stages of avocado production, a thorough cost analysis is helpful. This covers both variable expenditures that change with each harvest cycle and fixed costs like building infrastructure and purchasing land.

Avocado growers may effectively manage and distribute financial resources by creating a detailed budget. It includes estimating revenue, detailing costs, and establishing budgetary goals.

A well-organized budget enables farmers to maximize resource use, make well-informed decisions, and pinpoint areas where cost-cutting strategies can be applied. To adjust to shifting market conditions and unforeseen obstacles in avocado farming, budgetary monitoring and adjustments must be made continuously.

BUDGETING FOR AVOCADO PLANTATIONS

In avocado farming, financial planning is a strategic process that entails goal-setting, creating plans of action, and putting those plans into practice. To maintain the profitable and sustainable operation of their farms, avocado growers organize their finances. This entails determining if growing avocados is financially feasible, comprehending consumer trends, and matching supply to demand.

Risk management is an essential component of efficient financial planning in avocado cultivation. Farmers must identify possible risks, such as changes in the weather, illnesses, and market volatility, and then put procedures in place to lessen those risks. Financial planning commonly uses insurance products and revenue stream diversification to protect avocado farms from financial instability.

EVALUATING ROI (RETURN ON INVESTMENT)

One of the most important metrics for assessing the performance and profitability of avocado farming operations is Return on Investment (ROI). In avocado farming, return on investment (ROI) is calculated by taking into account the entire financial outlay, which includes capital costs as well as operating expenses, and comparing it to the profits produced from selling avocado produce. This analysis sheds light on how well and efficiently resources are used on the farm.

Avocado growers need to account for the growth cycle of their avocado trees when calculating return on investment (ROI), in addition to the revenue from avocado sales.

Based on the financial performance of their avocado farms, the ROI analysis assists farmers in making well-informed decisions about resource allocation, expansion, or diversification. In the fast-paced agriculture sector, producers can adjust their tactics and streamline their operations for long-term financial viability through routine ROI monitoring and assessment.

CHAPTER TEN

ORGANIC AND SUSTAINABLE AVOCADO FARMING

ADVANTAGES OF SUSTAINABLE AVOCADO PRODUCTION

There are several advantages to sustainable avocado production that go beyond environmental concerns. The preservation of natural resources is one of the main benefits. Farmers try to limit water use, prevent soil erosion, and maximize energy efficiency by implementing sustainable methods. Maintaining vital supplies, not only protects the fragile ecosystems around avocado plantations but also guarantees the industry's longevity.

Furthermore, by incorporating a variety of plants and commodities into their avocado orchards, farmers using sustainable farming practices frequently promote biodiversity growth and a more resilient and healthy ecosystem.

CERTIFICATION AND PRACTICES FOR ORGANIC PRODUCTS

To promote sustainable avocado farming, obtaining organic certification and adhering to organic agricultural methods are essential. Avocados farmed without the use of artificial pesticides, herbicides, or genetically modified organisms (GMOs) are guaranteed by organic certification. Eliminating the harmful effects of conventional farming pesticides, not only preserves consumer health but also the environment. Prioritizing soil health, organic avocado farming depends on crop rotation and natural fertilizers to preserve nutrient balance and increase the ecosystem's overall resilience.

FULFILLING CUSTOMER DEMAND FOR ECO-FRIENDLY PRODUCTS

Growing consumer demand for sustainable products has made the agricultural sector—which includes avocado farming—more competitive. Avocados farmed sustainably are in high demand as customers place a higher value on morality and environmental responsibility. In addition to gaining more access to markets, farmers who meet this need also help create a positive feedback loop that makes sustainable farming practices more popular and profitable. The sustainability of avocado farming as a whole is further supported by producers' adoption of more ecologically friendly techniques as a result of this shift in consumer preferences.

A crucial element of sustainable avocado cultivation is the application of water-saving techniques. Because avocado trees require a lot of water, sustainable methods are essential in areas where there is a risk of drought or water scarcity.

Avocado farming may be sustained over the long term by farmers using practices like drip irrigation, rainwater collection, and soil moisture monitoring to optimize water usage and minimize environmental effects.

Sustainable avocado farming reduces the ecological impact of water-intensive crops by using water resources properly.

An additional essential component of sustainable avocado production is integrated pest management. Farmers use a holistic approach to pest management that includes companion planting, natural predators, and other non-chemical techniques rather than depending solely on chemical pesticides. This reduces the negative effects on the environment and contributes to the upkeep of a healthy ecosystem that supports the growth of beneficial creatures. Sustainable pest control techniques improve the general well-being of the avocado orchard and its surroundings.

The advantages of environmentally conscious avocado cultivation go well beyond preserving the environment. Farmers may meet the increasing demand from consumers for sustainable products by adopting organic certification and methods. This improves market accessibility while simultaneously supporting the sustainability and long-term viability of avocado production. Sustainable avocado farming allows for an integrated approach that takes into account consumer and ecological concerns through integrated pest management, water conservation, and responsible resource management.

www.ingramcontent.com/pod-product-compliance
Lightning Source LLC
Chambersburg PA
CBHW072250310526
45795CB00011B/855